How to Make a Website or Blog with WordPress WITHOUT Coding

Plus an introduction to online entrepreneurship, passive income websites, and how making money online *actually* works!

By Mike Omar

This ebook was brought to you by
http://makemoneyfromhomelionsclub.com.

If you are interested in entrepreneurship, making passive income online, and other ways to make money outside of a standard job, be sure to visit http://makemoneyfromhomelionsclub.com!

In the first video lesson you are taught the entire process of how http://mikeomarphotography.com was made from beginning to end, without the need of any coding knowledge, in under one hour!

With the lessons taught there, you will be able to make yourself a professional website with any kind of look that you want.

There are also lessons on Search Engine Optimization (SEO), social media promotion, making mailing lists, selling ebooks and other digital products, developing passive income online, and more. There are also lessons on how to make money with Google, Amazon, and ClickBank (all passive!).

Note: All of the links within this book can be found easily from my main website: http://makemoneyfromhomelionsclub.com

I love connecting with my readers and something I like to do is personally help them with their online financial goals.

I'd be happy to help you find success in any way that I can.

Please feel free to send me an email telling me who you are, why you are interested in making money online, what your online income goals are, and how you found out about my online school. You can email me via the "contact" page of the LIONS CLUB website.

You can find all of my ebooks at http://makemoneyfromhomelionsclub.com/amazon

Mike Omar

My books:

HOW TO MAKE A WEBSITE OR BLOG: with WordPress WITHOUT Coding, on your own domain, all in under 2 hours. http://makemoneyfromhomelionsclub.com/ebook1

HOW TO MAKE MONEY ONLINE: Learn how to make money from home with my step-by-step plan to build a $5000 per month passive income website portfolio (based on building 10 websites that make at least $500 per month each). http://makemoneyfromhomelionsclub.com/ebook

HOW TO START A BLOG THAT PEOPLE WILL READ: How to create a website, write about a topic you love, develop a loyal readership, and make six figures doing it. http://makemoneyfromhomelionsclub.com/ebookblog

All of the following websites were made using the exact same techniques outlined in this book and video lessons. Any of these websites will be within your ability to create once you complete the lessons:

Make Money from Home LIONS CLUB – http://makemoneyfromhomelionsclub.com – My main website.

Mike Omar Photography – http://mikeomarphogoraphy.com – My freelancing website where I used to make websites for clients at $500 each (now it simply serves as an example website).

$1,000 / Month Passive Income Website – http://makemoneyfromhomesamplewebsite.com - This is the structure and layout of a $1,000 / Month Passive Income website monetized with with Google Adsense and Amazon Associates.

Sample Sales Page – http://makemoneyfromhomeinfoproduct.com – A samples sales page template that teaches how to make a website designed to sell a digital product.

How to Become a Ticket Broker – http://howtobecomeaticketbroker.net - A live example of one of my passive income websites that makes money selling a digital product (an ebook).

High Quality Outsourcing – http://highqualityoutsourcing.com - If you are interested in outsourcing the entire SEO backlinking process through my personal team (to get high rankings for your website(s) for specific keywords in Google and other searches), you can learn about that service here.

A few important things to keep in mind while reading through this book:

Throughout the book you will be referred to video lessons. While everything in the book and video lessons is as up to date as possible (I frequently update this book and the video lessons), the place to check for the most up-to-date information is in the *video descriptions* (on the same page you watch the videos). This can be the video descriptions on the pages of the LIONS CLUB website, or the video description of wherever you are watching the videos. Be sure to read the video descriptions of each video *before* watching the video itself.

Also, in this book you will find a lot of concepts are repeated. I know some readers will find this somewhat annoying, but several of my readers have told me they really like this because it really reinforces the most important concepts to take away from this book. That is why the book is written this way.

And most important of all: don't forget to sign up for my free weekly LIONS CLUB newsletter. Not only will you get great information with advice on how to make money online and how to build an online business, it is also where I send out updates regarding ranking strategies, new traffic generation techniques, important announcements, etc. Please sign up here:

http://makemoneyfromhomelionsclub.com/newsletter

Table of Contents

Introduction 8
How to Buy a Domain(s) and Hosting 11
Installing WordPress 16
An Introduction to WordPress and Best Search Engine
Optimization (SEO) Settings for your Website............................20
How to Change the Look of Your Website by Choosing Different
Themes 24
How to Add Posts / Pages, Pictures, and Links............................26
How to Set Up the Sidebar Using Widgets 31
How to Add Plugins like a Contact Form, an XML sitemap, and
Social Media Buttons 34
How to set up a Mailing List / Automated Newsletter and Best
Practices..38
Advanced WordPress Manipulation................................41
    Installing Google Analytics and Tracking 41
    How to Add "Buy Now" PayPal Buttons..................................41
    Adding an Interactive Google Maps to Your Website 42
    Resources: Ecommerce, Keyword Research, Link Building,
    Affiliate Marketing, Membership Websites, Outsourcing, Video
    Recording, and more..42
An Introduction to Making Money Online....................................43
    What are some of the most common methods for making money
    online? 43
    What is the simplest way to make passive money online?........48
    If I want to make money online, where do I start? 50
    The Structure of a $1,000 per Month Passive Income Website 54

Introduction

The ability to make a website is one of the most fundamental skills to have in today's modern world, and it has only become more important as time goes on. These days EVERYBODY needs a website.

Luckily it is not the 1990's, where the only way to make a website is by building it manually by writing lots and lots of code (after spending years learning different coding languages), only to go insane because your website won't do you what you want it to! Anyone who has been through this process knows what I'm talking about – programming for hours can be extremely frustrating!

Now we live in the era of WordPress. For those of you that have never heard of WordPress, it is a content management system that makes it extremely easy to build and update websites on your own domain.

Note: When I say we will be creating a website using WordPress, I don't mean creating one through the WordPress website. Websites created through there are severely limited in what you can do with them and offer very little flexibility overall. The method I teach enables you to create truly professional websites by installing the WordPress software and you won't be limited in any way.

Let me put it this way: if you can use Microsoft Word, you can build and maintain a website using WordPress! And there is no need of coding knowledge at all to do it!

Over *15%* of all websites on the Internet were made and currently operate with WordPress!

What kind of websites can you build with WordPress? Blogs, professional business websites, ecommerce websites, membership websites, social media websites, the list goes on and on!

To install WordPress on a domain you own doesn't take more than

15 minutes, and someone who knows what they are doing can make a professional website in less than one hour.

Set aside one hour and make your first website TODAY!

The point of today's exercise is simply for you to get your feet wet and to get a website online that you can play and experiment with. Don't worry too much about what this first website is going to be about; just get *something online*. After you complete this first project and feel comfortable with the process of putting together a professional looking website, *then* you can start building the rest of your websites.

If you don't know what to make your first website about, a fun first project could be building a website for your new side business: freelancing websites for others. After all, once you're done with the first four lessons, you'll be qualified to build fairly basic, but professional looking websites. Then start charging people $500 per website to make yourself some extra money! When I first learned how to make a website with WordPress, I used to post my services on http://craigslist.org daily, and I would get at least two to three gigs per month. You could simply make your website YourName.com or YourNameWebsiteCreationServices.com. If you decide to go this route, here is some freelancing advice to help you get started: http://mikeomarphotography.com/freelancing-advice/

You can also make yourself a blog about your favorite hobby or one that follows your experiences with building an online business - personal blogs that develop a regular readership make A LOT of money.

Remember: every day you don't start your blog, money is being left on the table.

You can also make yourself a blog about your favorite hobby or one that follows your experiences with building an online business - personal blogs that develop a regular readership make A LOT of money. Remember: every day you don't start

your blog, money is being left on the table.

Once you have gone through this book entirely, you will be a qualified freelance web designer, since most websites will be within your ability to design!

I charge $500 per website to clients, which:

1) is MUCH cheaper than my competitors
2) means I make about $250 per hour!

What should the domain name of your first website be? http://YourNameWebsiteDesignServices.com (or something along those lines).

OR http://YourNameLearnsToMakeMoneyOnline.com (or something along those lines).

Want to know what mine is? http://mikeomarphotography.com :)

Note: all the lessons in this book can also be found on http://makemoneyfromhomelionsclub.com in video form!

How to Buy a Domain(s) and Hosting

The following lessons on how buy a domain, buy a hosting account, connect the two accounts, and install WordPress can also be found in video form on this page: http://makemoneyfromhomelionsclub.com/lesson-1-1-how-to-make-a-website-or-blog-without-coding-using-wordpress/

I suggest you watch that video in addition to the reading below.

There are two things you need to buy in order to own and operate a live website: the domain and the hosting. The domain of the website is the URL or the website address (i.e. http://www.example.com). A standard domain will cost you about $15 / year.

The hosting is where all the information and content of your website is stored. This information is stored on a server somewhere (a server is basically a giant computer) and you pay to rent out some of the space. A standard hosting package will cost you about $10 - $20 / month. Those are the bare essential costs associated with owning and operating a live portfolio of websites (and therefore, an online business).

A good place to buy both of these products is Black Steel Hosting. They offer any available domain names and high quality hosting at a good price and offer 24 / 7 tech support (which is really nice to have whenever things go wrong and you aren't a technical person, like me!).

To start the process of registering a domain and hosting, first click here: http://makemoneyfromhomelionsclub.com/blacksteelhosting

You can also find a link to their website under my resources page here:

http://makemoneyfromhomelionsclub.com/resources

Just go to "Domain Registration and Hosting" and you will see a link to Black Steel Hosting there.

By the way, all my resources for building websites and developing an online passive income are on that page, so you should go ahead and bookmark it for future reference!

After clicking on the link, you will redirected to the Black Steel Hosting homepage. In the center of the screen there will be a blank box where you can type in any domain you are looking for. If you want to go ahead with the project of making yourself a website advertising your new business (freelance web design), go ahead and type in something like http://YourNameWebsites.com or http://YourNameWebsiteCreationServices.com, or something along those lines.

Note: Don't just read along without doing anything; actually build yourself a website now, even if it's just a practice one for fun!

Once you have typed in the domain you want, press the big green button "Search." If the name is available, at the next screen you will see it written in green; if it isn't, you will see it written in red. You can also get the same domain with other endings if you want (.net, .org, .biz, etc.).

Note: If you are interested in developing a brand for your domain, it might be a good idea to buy the .net and .org as well as the .com, even if you don't build anything on those domains (this is simply so nobody else can build a website there). You can just check off all the ones that you want and click on the drop down on the right to specify how long you would like to register each domain for. Once you are finished adding all the domains you want to your cart, press "Order now" to get to the next screen.

Note: If you are going to buy more domains, you'll have to get to the end of the checkout process to the "Order Summary" page, then press the "Continue Shopping" button instead of the "Checkout" button. There you can click on the "Register Domain" link to order more domains before checking out.

On the next screen "Domains Configuration", you have the option to add "ID Protection" to your domains. The way the Internet is set up, by default all websites publicly list the information of the owner (name, address, phone number, etc.). The only way to block this information from being publicly available is to add the "ID Protection." This will keep the owner's personal information anonymous and block people from being able to find it. Whether you get "ID Protection" for your websites or not is a personal preference, but I like to buy it for my websites.

The "Nameservers" below can be left as is and then press "Update Cart."

The next page is the checkout page, but we've only bought the domain(s) so far, so now we need to buy the hosting. Go ahead and click "Continue Shopping."

At the next screen you'll be taken directly to the "Web Hosting" link. Here you are going to pick between three levels of hosting (depending on your needs). The smallest package is for a single website, so if you know for a fact that you are building only one website, go for that one. The middle package can host up to 10 websites, and for most people reading this, that will be the appropriate package to get. If you are going to be building more than 10 websites, go for the largest package.

Once you select the hosting plan you want, click on "Order Now." On the next screen at "Product Configuration" click on the option "Use a domain already in my shopping cart" and then pick any of the domains you are buying from the drop down menu. The domain you pick will be the main one associated with your hosting account (although it doesn't matter which one you pick...just pick one). Then press "Click to Continue."

On the next screen you'll be at the "Product Configuration" page and can pick your billing cycle. The way the payment plans are set up, the longer you buy in advance, the cheaper the monthly price, so I'd go for at least a year.

Below that, you have the option of adding on the "Backup Restores Program" or "Professional Script Installation." The backups might be a good idea if you are not very tech savvy and would like to be able to have Black Steel Hosting back up your website to any previously saved backups (in case you mess something up). You also have the "Professional Script Installation" option available if you would like Black Steel Hosting to install WordPress on your domain(s) for you. If you opt for that option, you can skip the "Installing WordPress" chapter. :)

Once you are done, go ahead and press "Add to Cart" and continue on until you get to the final checkout page.

Before pressing "Checkout", some of you may need to get an SSL Certificate. SSL Certificates are for people who need to protect sensitive information that customers will be submitting through your website. Examples include any kind of website where people are submitting personal or credit card information to buy a product, or any kind of website where people are entering login details (membership websites / forums), or any kind of e-commerce website. For any websites like that, you'll need an SSL Certificate (to protect your customer's information).

If you don't need an SSL Certificate for any of your websites, go ahead and press the "Checkout" button and complete your order. If you do need an SSL certificate for any of your websites, click on the "Continue Shopping" button and then click on the "SSL Certificates" link.

Here you will find different levels of SSL Certificates available and can read the descriptions to figure out which one most suits your needs. Once you have picked the one you need, press the "Order Now" button and select the domain you want it for. Then proceed to the checkout page.

At the checkout page you can review your order and make sure everything looks good. If you need additional domains or want to add anything, just click on the "Continue Shopping" button. If you are all set, click on the "Checkout" button and pay for your products.

Note: Write down the password you create during the checkout process, as you will need it soon!

Once you've finished checking out, you'll get to a confirmation page, and you're all set!

Installing WordPress

The next step is to install WordPress on your domain(s.). First go back to the Black Steel Hosting website and click on the "Client Area" tab. Go ahead and login with your email address and the password you created during the checkout process.

From this area you'll be able to access the products you already own, buy more domains / addons, upgrade hosting, and open support tickets if you need technical support. This is your main "homebase" area where you will start to build your online business from. :)

Once you are logged in, go to the "My Products and Services" page (under "Services", then "My Services"). Your hosting account should be listed there, and then press the "View Details" button of your hosting account. Once you do that, click on the "Login to cPanel" button and a new page will open up.

Note: If your browser says "not safe, do not proceed" or something like that, just ignore it and continue to your cPanel.

Once you are at the cPanel, you're going to scroll down and click on the button that says "WordPress" under the "Softaculous Apps Installer" category. Then press "Install."

These are the options you should pick when installing WordPress:

Choose Protocol: http:// (or if you got SSL, then pick https://).

Choose Domain: Pick the domain you want to install WordPress on. At first, there will only be the domain that your hosting account is associated with. After installing this first one, I'll show you how to install WordPress on your other domains.

In Directory: Make it blank.

Database Name: Leave as is.

Table Prefix: Leave as is.

Site Name: Pick the name of your website (can be changed later).

Site Description: Pick a tagline for your website (can be changed later or left blank).

Enable Multisite (WPMU): Unchecked.

Admin Username: Pick something (but don't leave it as "admin"!).

Admin Password: Pick something (make it hard!) and write it down somewhere.

Admin Email: Your personal email is fine (can be changed later).

Select Language: This is your preference.

Limit Login Attempts: I would recommend checking this. This installs a plugin that helps prevent brute attacks of people trying to figure out your username and password by temporarily blocking people who have messed up the login information three times in a row.

Under the "Advanced Options" area (these can be chosen based on personal preference, but I wrote down my preferences below):

Disable Update Notifications: Unchecked.

Auto Upgrade: Checked.

Auto Upgrade WordPress Plugins: Unchecked.

Auto Upgrade WordPress Themes: Unchecked.

Automated Backups: Once a week.

Backup Rotation: 4

Then press the "Install" button.

WordPress should now be installed on your website! If you type in your domain into your web browser, you should see a plain looking website without any actual information on it except for your website title and a "Hello world!" announcement in the middle; that is the default WordPress installation.

If you are NOT seeing the default WordPress installation, there are a couple of things you can try first before contacting technical support:

1. Clear the cache on your browser and then reload your website. If you don't know how to do this, just search how in Google with whatever browser you're using (for example search for: how to clear cache on browser Google Chrome or how to clear cache on browser Internet Explorer). It should only take a few minutes to clear your cache. Once you do this, try reloading your website to see if you now have the default WordPress installation on there.

2. Wait some time. Sometimes it takes a while for the whole process to complete with the new domain connecting to the servers and then the installation process. It supposedly can take up to 24 hours for all of this to complete, but I've never seen it take longer than a couple of hours.

Note: To add WordPress to other domains within your account, you have to do one additional step. Within your cPanel, go to "Addon Domains" under the "Domains" category. Once inside, type your domain in the "New Domain Name" box (you must have already purchased this domain earlier and it must be within your Black Steel Hosting account).

In the "Subdomain or FTP Username" box, pick a username and write it down somewhere.

In the "Document Root" box, the information should have auto-filled in after you typed in your "New Domain Name", so just leave it as is. Then pick your password (make it hard!) and also write it down somewhere. Then press the "Add Domain" button and you are set.

Now start the exact same process as earlier, by scrolling down to the "WordPress" button under the "Softaculous Apps Installer" category. :)

An Introduction to WordPress and Best Search Engine Optimization (SEO) Settings for your Website

Note: You can watch me login to WordPress and modify the settings on the video lesson on the following page:

http://makemoneyfromhomelionsclub.com/lesson-1-2-how-to-add-pages-posts-widgets-a-sidebar-and-new-themes-to-your-wordpress-installation/

Anytime you need to modify or update your website, you will have to log in to the back end of your website, which can be done directly from your web browser.

What you do is type in http://YourDomainName.com/wp-login and at that screen, type in your username and password that you set up when you were installing WordPress. This will take you to the back end of WordPress.

If you were already logged in, typing in that URL will take you directly to the backend of WordPress.

The backend of WordPress will look something like this (depending on what version of WordPress you have installed):

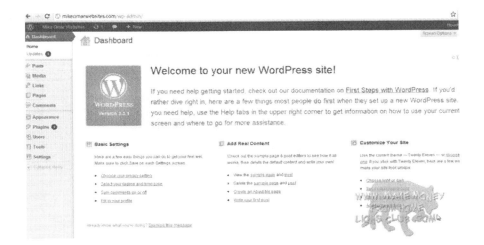

Note: Always be sure you are working with the latest version of WordPress available! This will help keep your website secure and running smoothly. Anytime you log in to your website, it will alert you on the main screen if your WordPress installation is not up to date, and if it isn't, all you have to do is follow the instructions on the screen for it to self-install the latest version. It is as simple as clicking a few buttons right there on the main screen to update to the latest version!

Note 2: Don't be afraid to mess around with the settings all over the back end, and then refresh the website on another tab to see what changed or updated – all errors can be undone and this is a great way to familiarize yourself with the back end of WordPress.

The first thing you want to do when you get to the back end is update some of the settings (although most of the settings will be kept the same, since the default settings are usually what you want). The way to update the settings options is to go to "Settings" on the left sidebar, and click on the subcategory that you want to modify. Here are the most important ones to familiarize yourself with and update (although you should still take a look at the others to see what they are).

Settings: General: At this screen you can update your site title, add a tagline if you wish, and the email address you want emails to be sent to (related to your website updates, alerts, etc.). The settings should already be filled out with the information you typed in when installing the initial WordPress installation, but this is where you would go if you ever needed to make any updates to that.

Settings: Reading: Here you can decide what page or post(s) you want to display on the homepage. This could either be your latest blog posts (if you are building a blog), a static post that you always want on the homepage (maybe your most popular blog article), or a a static page (maybe for a standard website instead of a blog). We will go over posts and pages later, but this is where you set what goes on your homepage.

Settings: Discussion: Here you can update the options for commenting on blog posts. If you have a blog and want to encourage discussions, you can allow people to comment on your posts, and then decide if those comments automatically appear or if you have to approve them first. If you have a standard business or informational website and don't want the option for commenting to appear, you can turn that option off in this section, and people won't have the option to comment.

Settings: Permalinks: Permalinks is how the URL of a new page or post is determined. In other words, if you write a new post, what is the URL of the post going to be? This is an important one for Search Engine Optimization (SEO) purposes, and it's something you want to update before you start doing anything else.

When you go to this page, make sure the setting is on "post name" instead of the default. This will make sure that all your URLs have nice keywords in there, instead of the default version that would make all your URLs look something like this:

http://YourDomainName.com/?p=123

Once you make this update, if you make an "about me" page, the URL will automatically save as this:

http://YourDomainName.com/about-me

Now that you have optimized your settings, let's go over how to modify the look of your website by adding different themes.

How to Change the Look of Your Website by Choosing Different Themes

Note: You can watch me change the themes of a WordPress website on the video lesson on the following page:

http://makemoneyfromhomelionsclub.com/lesson-1-2-how-to-add-pages-posts-widgets-a-sidebar-and-new-themes-to-your-wordpress-installation/

WordPress makes it really easy to update and switch up the look of your website by being able to easily add themes or replace the theme that your website is currently using – all without messing up the data you have on your website already.

There are literally thousands of different free themes available online, and a huge number of them can be accessed directly from your WordPress back end. To add new themes (and you can add as many as you want and switch between them easily), simply go to the sidebar on the left and click on "appearance" and then click on the subcategory "themes."

Once there, press the tab at the top that says "Install Themes." The screen should look like this:

Once you are at this screen, you can simply press the "search" button and it will display all kinds of free themes for you to choose from. If you are looking for a theme with specific colors or features, simply check off those boxes and then press "search."

Once you press "search" you will be taken to the results page, which will show you each theme you can pick from with three different options for each: "details", "preview", and "install now." Clicking on details will give you a short description of the theme and its features. Clicking on preview will show you what your website would look like if you installed that theme on it (with your settings, posts, pages, etc. all transferred over). Clicking on "install now" will actually change the theme for you.

Go ahead and pick one you like and click "install now." When you go to refresh your website, you should see that your entire website has been updated with your new theme. Feel free to look around for a while and try out some different themes!

Note: If you are trying to create a *professional* looking blog or website, I would recommend looking into using premium themes designed by professional web designers (all my major websites use premium themes). They aren't expensive, are highly customizable in ways that free themes usually aren't, and will greatly increase the credibility of your blog or website.

The best resources for affordable premium WordPress themes can be found on the following page under "Premium Themes":

http://makemoneyfromhomelionsclub.com/resources

How to Add Posts / Pages, Pictures, and Links

Note: You can watch me add posts, pages, pictures, and links on the video lesson on the following page:

http://makemoneyfromhomelionsclub.com/lesson-1-2-how-to-add-pages-posts-widgets-a-sidebar-and-new-themes-to-your-wordpress-installation/

Posts and pages are where you will add all the "meat" of your websites – all the content! Posts and pages are almost identical in terms of how to publish them: the only real difference is their purpose and where they are displayed on your website.

Pages are generally the static informational pages of your website that go along the top navigational bar – things like "about us", "contact us", "terms and conditions", "FAQs", "privacy policy", etc. They can generally be accessed from any page on your website since they are part of the main navigation.

Posts are generally for bloggers where people are writing new entries periodically. They are usually dated and categorized, and are usually the parts of a website where people can leave comments and discuss things.

If you go to "Pages" on the left sidebar on the back end, you will see two subcategories: "All pages" and "Add new." At all pages you can see the pages that are currently live, and you can edit them or delete them as you wish.

Since this is a new website, you don't have any pages yet, so go to "Add new" to add a new page. At this page you will see that there are plenty of buttons and options for adding a new page, but it is really not that different from buttons you would see on Microsoft Word. The screen looks like this:

For the title of page, enter it where it says "Enter title here." In the big text box below, you can type away anything and everything you want (and as you can see, you have font and formatting options in the toolbar). When you are satisfied with your entry, press the blue "publish" button on the right, and your page will go live!

Go ahead and add a few pages and publish them, and then refresh your website so you can see it updated with the new pages on there.

For adding posts, the process is exactly the same, except you can add categories and tags as well. Go to the left sidebar and press "Posts", and then press "Add new" and you will end up at a screen that is nearly identical to the "Add new" screen for pages:

On this screen, however, you will see two new boxes on the right: "tags" and "categories."

For those of you that haven't heard of tags, tags are defined as:

"Tags provide a useful way to group related posts together and to quickly tell readers what a post is about. Tags also make it easier for people to find your content."

Adding tags is completely optional (I don't use them on my websites, but a lot of people do).

You can also categorize your posts as well, selecting the category (or categories) you want your post to be in (done in the "category" box on the right). You can also add new categories to your blog / website directly on this screen.

Go ahead and add a few posts and categories and refresh your website so you can see where they are placed.

Note: If you don't see them, that simply means that your theme doesn't have them display as the default setting, so you'll have to do it manually with widgets. Widgets are how your set up the sidebar, and we can have the website display (or not display) posts and / or categories there (all of that is taught in the next chapter).

Now it is time to get a little fancy, and learn how to add pictures and links to our pages / posts! Adding pictures and links is done directly on the post or page you want to add them to.

To add a picture, press on the button next to "upload / insert" right above the entry text tool bar (because it is a little hard to find, I circled it in red in the following screen shot):

Once you press this button, the next screen will ask you to either drag and drop a picture directly onto that screen, or press "select file" to pick a file from your computer to add to your post or page.

Once you have chosen the file, it will give you the option to give it a title, an alternate title (the text that displays when your mouse scrolls over an image when you are browsing the web), a caption, a description, a link URL (a place the picture will link to if you press on it), the alignment, and the size of the picture. Once you are happy with your settings, click on the "use this image" button, and the image will be inserted into your post or page.

Next time you update your post or page, the picture will display on your website! You can always come back and edit this image or delete it if you wish, by clicking on the image, and then pressing that same button to edit (or just the "delete" button on your keyboard to delete).

To add a link to a post or page is just as simple. Just highlight the word or words you want to convert into a link, and then press the link button (circled in red on the following screenshot):

Once you do that, the next screen will ask you what URL you would like to link the highlighted area to, so simply type it in. The "title" text box can be left blank, and if you would like the link to open in a new tab or window (instead of your current screen), check the box that says "Open link in a new window / tab."

Press "update" and your text will now be a link! Visit the page and test it out!

Next, it is time to learn how to set up the sidebar using widgets.

How to Set Up the Sidebar Using Widgets

Note: You can watch me set up the sidebar using widgets on the video lesson on the following page:

http://makemoneyfromhomelionsclub.com/lesson-1-2-how-to-add-pages-posts-widgets-a-sidebar-and-new-themes-to-your-wordpress-installation/

Setting up the sidebar with widgets is very simple to do. Go to the left sidebar on the back end and press "appearance" and then press the subcategory "widgets."

Here you will be taken to a screen that looks like this:

On the left side of the page there are all the different types of widgets, and on the right side of the page are the widget areas, where the widgets can be dragged over and dropped in (in any order you want). In this theme, there is only one widget area (titled "Right Sidebar"), but different themes have different set-ups (some have several widget areas, like "footer", etc.). They all work the same way though – a drag and drop system.

In the screen shot above, we can see that within the "Right Sidebar" widget area, there are five different widgets that have been dragged in ("Text: Brought to you by:", "The Social Links",

"Pages", "Text: Purchase a Website", and "Text: Sign up...").

Now look at the screen shot of the website on the front end:

As you can see, on the right sidebar are those same widgets, displayed in the same order. To modify the widget, you can do that directly within the drop-down menu of the widget itself on the back end screen (each widget has its own options).

The back end is a simple drag and drop process to edit the order of the sidebar (or other widget areas), and you modify the widgets themselves on that screen as well. To get rid of a widget, simply drag it out of the widget area, and it will disappear.

Here is a quick rundown of the most important widgets:

Text: This widget is the most versatile, because it allows you to add any text that you want, or insert any code that you want, and it will display on the main website. The text widget is HTML based. For example, the top widget on my website is a text image titled "Brought to you by:" and it has the logo of http://makemoneyfromhomelionsclub.com that links to that website.

I simply added the HTML code into that widget (HTML lessons are for another book, but if you ever need HTML code help, just type "how to add a picture link in HTML" into Google, and it will show you how to do it – that's how I learned!). If you were to add basic text into that widget like "Welcome to my website!", that is what would display on the website.

Same thing goes for adding links to your sidebar (you'll have to add them in HTML code). Just type in "HTML link" into Google (or "HTML link blank" into Google for links that you'd like to open in a new tab). The code that shows up is what you would put in the text widget. For example:

```
<a href="http://www.example.com/">Anchor Text</a>
```

OR

```
<a href="http://www.example.com/" target="_blank">Anchor Text</a>
```

This HTML code is for a link that will open in a new tab.

Pages: Add the pages widget and all your pages will be displayed on the sidebar (like shown in the screen shot above).

Recent Posts: Add the posts widget and all your latest posts will be displayed on the sidebar (with options about how many are shown, etc.).

Like with the other sections of this book, I recommend you play around with this area a little bit. Add and remove widgets and modify them as you wish, and then refresh the website to see how it looks. As you are starting to realize, WordPress is very versatile and you have a lot of options on how your website looks beyond what theme you picked.

How to Add Plugins like a Contact Form, an XML sitemap, and Social Media Buttons

Note: You can watch me adding plugins on the video lesson on the following page:

http://makemoneyfromhomelionsclub.com/lesson-1-3-how-to-add-social-media-buttons-a-contact-form-google-maps-and-paypal-buttons/

Plugins are one of the coolest features of WordPress because they enable you to do SO much with your website – all without having to write any of the code yourself! Plugins are pieces of software designed by freelancers that you can install directly on your website (similar to how you install themes) that enable you to do all kinds of neat things – virtually anything! They are kind of like "apps" that you download for smartphones, only they are for your website instead.

Here are just a few examples of what plugins can do for your website: add a contact form, add social media buttons, add image sliders, add subscription features, add ecommerce stores, add a forum...the list goes on and on! It is really almost anything you can think of.

To install widgets, click on "Plugins" on the left sidebar of the back end, and then click "add new." Then in the "search" text box, search for the features for a plugin you would like to add to your website, and then click the "search plugins" button.

For example, if there is anything you want your website to do (as in, you think to yourself "I'd really like to add social share buttons to my website pages and posts"), then you could type in "social share buttons" and click "search plugins."

When I did that, I got these results:

As you can see, the results actually have star-ratings so you can see what other people have rated those plugins (remember, these are made by freelancers, so these plugins can be far from perfect!). The star rating is a pretty good metric though, and anything that has four stars or more that fits what I'm looking for, I'll usually install and test out to see if I like it.

The example I used above is actually what I did when looking for a cool plugin to add social buttons to my websites, and I ended up going with the one titled "Slick Social Share Buttons" in the screen shot above. Once the plugin is installed and configured, it displays on the website like this (circled in red):

Doesn't that look professional? This would have been a nightmare to program on my own, but with plugins, it took less than 10 minutes. THAT is the power of plugins.

After you have found the plugin you want to install in the search results, simply press "install now." Once it is installed, the next screen will ask you if you want to activate the plugin (press "activate plugin").

At this point, some plugins are installed automatically and you're finished, and others need one more step, which is to be configured. If a plugin needs to be configured, you can usually find a new settings button for that plugin on the left sidebar of the back end, or sometimes you can find that button under the "settings" button of the left sidebar. Different plugins are placed in different areas of the back end, depending on how the programmer designed it, and you have to find them and configure them (not hard to do). Also, all the plugins usually have a website linked from the plugins page with screen shots, explanations of how to use the plugins, and FAQs.

Like I said, this is the part that is the trickiest (messing around with plugins and getting them to work), but considering the pay off, they are certainly worth installing and playing with!

Here are some of my top recommended plugins and what they do:

Slick Social Share Buttons – This is the plugin I just talked about that installs those cool share buttons on any pages and posts that you want.

I actually show the installation and configuration of that plugin on the video that is on this page:

http://makemoneyfromhomelionsclub.com/lesson-1-3-how-to-add-social-media-buttons-a-contact-form-google-maps-and-paypal-buttons/

Contact Form 7 – This plugin allows you to easily install one of those contact forms where people fill in their information if they want to contact you (instead of you just listing an email address where they can reach you). It makes your website look a little more professional and it allows you to not publicly display your email address. I show you the installation and configuration of that contact form on that same page I just mentioned:

http://makemoneyfromhomelionsclub.com/lesson-1-3-how-to-add-social-media-buttons-a-contact-form-google-maps-and-paypal-buttons/

Google XML Sitemaps – This plugin automatically generates an XML sitemap for you, which helps Google, Bing, Yahoo, and Ask index your website for their search engines. In plain English, it helps search engines find your website and alerts them of updates immediately!

All-in-One SEO Pack – This is the best plugin to be able to configure your website titles so that it is fully Search Engine Optimized (SEO'd). I give a full tutorial on how to best install and configure this plugin on the following two pages:

http://makemoneyfromhomelionsclub.com/lesson-3-1-how-to-make-a-2000-per-month-passive-income-website-using-onsite-seo-pt-1/

http://makemoneyfromhomelionsclub.com/lesson-3-2-how-to-make-a-2000-per-month-passive-income-website-using-onsite-seo-pt-2/

How to set up a Mailing List / Automated Newsletter and Best Practices

Note: You can watch me set up a mailing list and newsletter on the video lesson on the following page:

http://makemoneyfromhomelionsclub.com/lesson-8-1-how-to-set-up-a-mailing-list-and-autoresponder-newsletter-with-aweber/

* Don't forget to sign up for the 100% free LIONS CLUB weekly newsletter on my website (it also serves as a live example of what I teach here)!

No website (or Facebook fan page, etc.) is complete until it has a sign up form to collect email addresses (otherwise, you're leaving money on the table). Every business in the world should have an email list, as well as a newsletter they send out on a regular basis. No matter what kind of online website you have (business website, personal blog, etc.), get a sign up form on there and start collecting emails immediately (even if you don't have a clear idea of what you're going to do with that mailing list yet). One of the most common regrets of anyone with an online presence is "not having started collecting emails sooner."

Here are a few of the advantages to having an emailing list:

- Your mailing list will never die, no matter what might happen to your website or business.
- The newsletter is a constant reminder of your business / services / etc.
- It is a much more personal way of communicating with your audience.
- It is the most effective way to communicate with your entire audience at once about time sensitive issues (announcements, special promotions, contests, etc.).

Here are a few important tips you don't want to forget when setting up your emailing list:

- A Get your mailing list set up as soon as you start your blog and start collecting email addresses as soon as possible.
- A A great way to get people to subscribe to your newsletter is to promise them something really cool for signing up! This could be a free ebook, a special coupon, or anything else. For mine, I promise that the "thank you" page will make them laugh.
- A Tell them in the welcome email to "whitelist" your email address so that your newsletter doesn't get blocked by spam filters. Also include in the welcome email what they should expect from your newsletter.
- A Make sure your sign up form is somewhere prominent on your website: getting each visitor to sign up for your mailing list should be a top goal.
- A Employ the same strategy you do with your social networks: every time you publish a new post, take a few extra minutes to send out a newsletter with a link to the post to your subscriber list.
- A Your newsletter is a great platform to sell and promote products. However, don't sell or promote products in every newsletter you send, or your audience will get annoyed and unsubscribe. Do your selling and promotion sparingly.

Make sure sending useful and informative content is your top priority, and your audience will stay loyal and won't ever want to unsubscribe.

In the video lesson I teach you how to set up a mailing list and autoresponder newsletter. This includes how to do automated messages with preset time intervals, as well as one-time broadcasts. I go over how to set up an inbox sign up form and a lightbox sign up form (the one that pops up). I also go over best practices for setting your mailing list so you grow your list faster and build a loyal following.

To watch the video lesson, click here:

http://makemoneyfromhomelionsclub.com/lesson-8-1-how-to-set-up-a-mailing-list-and-autoresponder-newsletter-with-aweber/

Advanced WordPress Manipulation

Here I will go over some of the more advanced things you can do with WordPress, as well as some other random bits of useful information!

Installing Google Analytics and Tracking

Installing tracking software is extremely important for any webmaster, as it allows you to analyze all kinds of interesting data about your site visitors: where they came from, what pages are the most popular on your website, what keywords you are ranking for in search engines...the list goes on and on!

There are lots of programs for tracking your visitors, but one of the most powerful ones is Google Analytics – and it is completely free!

I show you how to set up a Google Analytics account and install it on your website here:

http://makemoneyfromhomelionsclub.com/lesson-4-1-everything-you-need-to-know-about-google-adsense/

How to Add "Buy Now" PayPal Buttons

If you want a simple way to charge clients directly on your website, it doesn't get much simpler than PayPal. They can pay you with their PayPal account or any major credit card, and that money gets deposited directly into your account. I show you how to set up a PayPal button in the following lesson:

http://makemoneyfromhomelionsclub.com/lesson-1-3-how-to-add-social-media-buttons-a-contact-form-google-maps-and-paypal-buttons/

Adding an Interactive Google Maps to Your Website

If you are a small business, chances are you'd like to add an interactive Google Maps to your website. The process is actually very simple, and I show you how to do that right here:

http://makemoneyfromhomelionsclub.com/lesson-1-3-how-to-add-social-media-buttons-a-contact-form-google-maps-and-paypal-buttons/

Resources: Ecommerce, Keyword Research, Link Building, Affiliate Marketing, Membership Websites, Outsourcing, Video Recording, and more...

There are endless tools for making extremely powerful (and profitable!) websites. For the best tools in each category, and explanations / tutorials for each one, please visit:

http://makemoneyfromhomelionsclub.com/resources/

Again: all my resources for building websites and developing an online passive income are on that page, so you should go ahead and bookmark it for future reference!

An Introduction to Making Money Online

Learning how to make a website is the first step to making money online, and after reading this book and making yourself a website from scratch, you should already be pretty good at it! You should order yourself some business cards with your new freelancing services website on there, and start charging people $500 per website to start making yourself some easy money!

And now that you know how to make a website, it is time to learn about internet marketing and start building yourself an online portfolio of passive income websites!

The following four chapters are actually the first four newsletters of my weekly LIONS CLUB newsletter (which I highly recommend you sign up for, since it is 100% free!). I put them in this book because I think they are a fantastic introduction to how building an online passive income website portfolio is actually accomplished. Enjoy!

What are some of the most common methods for making money online?

Freelancing - The first most basic way to make money online is by freelancing (in other words, getting paid to make websites for other people). It's the way I got started in this whole business. More and more people need websites on a daily basis, yet most people never even look into how to make a website at all. If they did, they would realize that putting up a basic website is a simple process that takes less than an hour total and requires no knowledge of coding at all. The very first lesson I teach on my website is the making of http://mikeomarphotography.com (all my lessons are free video lessons that I recorded and put up online).

If you want to make money online, you need to learn how to make a website, plain and simple. Your first website project may as well be a website advertising your new website-making skills!

If you are interested in freelancing websites, you can find advice on how to do that here: http://mikeomarphotography.com/freelancing-advice/

Blogging – Blogging is one of the most common methods for making money online today, and one of the easiest to get started with.

Blogs have the potential to be unbelievably powerful. Never in the history of mankind has such a valuable, simple, and inexpensive tool existed for exploring topics, sharing ideas, connecting with others, and building businesses.

I never dreamed that blogging would lead to more personal and business opportunities, financial success, and clarity of mind and purpose than anything else in my life…but it has.

Blogging, combined with the power of social media, is one of the most powerful tools for massive exposure that exists today…and it's virtually free.

Let me put it this way: Everyone *needs* to have a blog. The potential upside of having one is just too great to ignore.

Not only will a blog offer you opportunities in all kinds of unexpected and immeasurable ways, the writing will force you to organize your thoughts and analyze topics in ways that wouldn't be possible otherwise.

In other words: The benefits that come from blogging will surprise you…over and over again.

Once your blog has either **a)** consistent search engine traffic or **b)** an established and loyal readership (preferably both!), the potential for making money is huge. I cover the most basic monetization techniques for blogs in this very same newsletter.

Go ahead and make yourself a blog about your favorite hobby or one that follows your experiences with building an online business - personal blogs that develop a regular readership make A LOT of money.

Remember: every day you don't start your blog, money is being left on the table.

To learn how to start a blog *that people will read* in book form (how to create a website, write about a topic you love, develop a loyal readership, and make six figures doing it), click here:

http://makemoneyfromhomelionsclub.com/ebookblog

Google Adsense - This is the simplest monetization method for a passive income website. Basically, you put the Adsense code on your website, people click on the links, and you get paid for every click. Then you receive a check from Google at the end of the month depending on the number of clicks. Plain and simple (in my next newsletter I will explain the entire process behind how Google Adsense works and why Google is one of the richest and most powerful companies in the world).

This method USUALLY makes you the least amount of money of all passive monetization techniques (although in some cases it is the only viable option). That is why you make your initial monetization technique Adsense (to get a foundation eCPM with which to compare the rest of your results from testing).

Once you understand the process of keyword research and Search Engine Optimization (SEO), I show you how to make this sample passive income website: http://makemoneyfromhomesamplewebsite.com/ , a website that is primarily monetized with Google Adsense.

If you build lots of these types of websites, the amount of money you can make passively is pretty much limitless.

To learn how to build a $5,000 per month passive income website portfolio by building 10 of these websites, completely step-by-step in book form, click here:

http://makemoneyfromhomelionsclub.com/ebook

Amazon Associates, Commission Junction, and Other Affiliate Programs -With these programs, you put an affiliate link on your website (this is a link pointing to another website with your tracking ID on it). Then if someone clicks on that link, whatever they buy from that site, you get a commission on (the tracking cookies vary in length, but it could be anything they buy in the next 24 hours to anything they buy in the next 30 days depending on the program). This method is a little more complicated to make money from, but if you do it right, you can do VERY well. This is because so many people go to whatever website from your affiliate link to buy that one product you recommended, but then they decide to do some extra shopping and buy a whole bunch of stuff. That means you get commission on THE ENTIRE PURCHASE!

This method works best for websites where you recommend and review products OR websites where your search engine traffic is highly targeted (i.e. you rank #1 for "toaster ovens" and your website is a bunch of toaster oven reviews with links to Amazon where they can buy them). It also works on blogs you have where you have a regular readership that trusts your opinion and you recommend specific products (using your affiliate link). Websites that are monetized with affiliate links make a KILLING during Christmas (my Amazon websites will make me more in November, December, and January than they do the rest of the year).

Informational Product Websites - These are websites where you sell your own downloadable product. This could be an book, software, a video series, or any other product. Basically if you are an expert in any field that people are looking for information on, you can put together an information product on it (and use whatever medium works best - for making money online, a video series works best). Then put up a website that tells people why the

46

product you made has value. You can use something like PayPal to charge for your product and then redirect them to a download page after, so it is pretty much a hands-free operation.

There are several third party credit card processing companies you can use to do this (including PayPal), but I personally like to use ClickBank and this is why: ClickBank allows other people to become an affiliate for you very easily. This means that other people can send traffic to my website, and if that person buys a product, I give them a portion of the profit. I like to participate in this program for all my informational product websites and give affiliates a generous 75% commission. I like to participate in the affiliate program because even though I'm giving up a portion of the profits, those are sales I wouldn't have had otherwise. It's a win-win.

On my website, in the more advanced lessons, I teach you the entire creation of this sample digital product sales page website: http://makemoneyfromhomeinfoproduct.com/ . My very first book website that I put up years ago was "How to Become a Ticket Broker": http://howtobecomeaticketbroker.net/ , and it continues to make me passive income to this day.

Membership Websites - Membership sites are probably the most complicated ones to start and become successful with, but if you can gain some momentum, these websites will make you the easiest and most consistent money out of any of them! This is basically a website where each member has to pay a monthly fee to gain access. If you charge $30/month to be a member of your website and you have 100 members, that's a steady $3,000 per month, and depending on the type of site you run, you may not have to do anything but maintenance (and you'd probably want to promote too, for more easy money...I mean members!). Include a forum within the website (not hard to do with a WordPress plugin) and some kind of service that keeps them wanting to stay members, and you're set - your new focus becomes getting more members while maintaining the site. And you can offer an affiliate program too so current members can send you new members that you wouldn't have gotten otherwise.

Those are some of the most common ways for making money online that don't involve shipping physical products (which are **E-commerce Websites** - yet ANOTHER method for making money online!). The possibilities for making money online are truly endless.

What is the simplest way to make passive money online?

Everyone knows that there is LOTS of money being made online by people all around the world on a daily basis. Every year the amount of money made online grows exponentially and hasn't showed any sign of slowing down, even during this terrible recession. And even though everyone knows that money is being made online, they don't understand HOW money is being made online.

So how exactly are people making money online?

To understand one method of making money online, let's examine one of the most profitable companies in the world: Google. Google commands the most search engine traffic in the world, and as a result is in a very powerful position. Why?

Well let's pretend that we are Nike. Because we are Nike, we want our website to rank #1 for shoes. If we rank #1 for shoes, we are going to get a lot of traffic for people searching for shoes to our website (roughly 42% of searchers to be exact). If we rank #2, we will only get about 25% of that traffic. At #3, about 10%. After that, the numbers start to get pretty low. You may as well not even exist on the Internet if you are on page #2 of the search results.

The exact search item "shoes" is searched for roughly 1,160,000 times per month. If Nike is at rank #1 in Google and getting 42% of that traffic, that is going to translate into almost 500,000 visitors to the Nike website that are interested in the word "shoes". That is going to translate into A LOT of sales. If it is sitting in spot #3, that would be a little over 100,000 visitors. Still a lot of sales, but MUCH lower. If they aren't in the top 10, they are missing out on a lot of action, and their company will miss out on a lot of potential sales.

And because Google controls where a website ranks, they are in a position of power. If they decide that Adidas is a more relevant search result for shoes than Nike is, Adidas will make much more money online than Nike does on the Internet. And Google has that power over every industry in the world!

So how does that ranking power translate into money for Google? Well, if you ever search for anything in Google, you may notice that the top two or three results have a slightly differently colored background. This is because those are paid search results (as opposed to the natural results below them, which are referred to as organic results). These top (differently colored) results are paid for by those companies so that their links can rank at the top of Google search engine results. Google is basically a lead generator to lots and lots of companies around the world. And whenever a regular searcher clicks on one of those paid links, the owner of that link pays Google for that click.

With millions of searches every single day, Google pulls in A LOT of money. And it makes sense that companies would pay for links, and this is why: Let's say that you are Nike and you know that 1 out of every 50 people that searches for "shoes" online will buy a pair of shoes if they land on www.nike.com. With this knowledge, you can calculate how much you could spend on a Pay-Per-Click (PPC) campaign with Google and be profitable. If the average pair of shoes makes Nike a $50 profit and each click costs an average of $.50, then out of every 50 clicks you pay for, at least one pair of shoes will sell, and therefore you will make a $25 profit (you paid $25 for 50 leads and made $50 profit off of the sale). In other words, if the leads from Google cost you less than amount of profit from those leads, it makes sense to set up a PPC campaign with Google and get your links on the top of the search results.

And Google just pulls in the money from all the companies out there that are doing this, even if it's just a dollar or two at a time (don't forget how many searches there are per day on Google though).

So how does this translate to regular people like ourselves making money online?

Well Google has a program called Google Adsense which allows website owners to put those same paid links on their own websites. And when someone clicks on one of those links on one of those websites, that company pays Google, and then Google pays the website owner a portion of that money.

Therefore, the first step to making a passive income online is to make a website that generates traffic, and the most basic way to monetize that traffic is with Google Adsense.

This is the foundation of everything I teach on my video lessons blog: how to generate free traffic to your websites and how to monetize that traffic. The simplest monetization method to implement is Google Adsense, but eventually I will teach you other monetization techniques for you to test that can result in much higher eCPM (earnings per thousand impressions!).

If I want to make money online, where do I start?

I have been making money off the Internet for several years now and have had many websites fail and many websites succeed (succeed meaning they make money passively, fail meaning they don't do anything). Now that I understand how the system works, I understand one of the biggest factors to building a successful website: doing proper research before even starting the process of building a website!

Many people (myself included, when I was a beginner) go about trying to make money online in the wrong order; they have an idea and then build a website based on this idea and then later on hope it pays off. This can cause many hours of work and frustration for a project that never makes a cent, and will cause a lot people to give up on their dream of making money online forever.

What would the correct sequence of action when starting a website to make money online?

Do your research first! What exactly do I mean by that?

Google provides the data for how many times every word (also known as a "keyword") is searched for around the world on a monthly basis. If you go into Google and search for the "Google Keyword Tool," you will be able to look up any keyword you can think of and see how many times it is searched for on a daily basis.

UPDATE: Google got rid of the Google Keyword Tool and replaced it with the Google Keyword Planner. Luckily, the new tool also provides the information we need!

You can also look up the value of that keyword if it is used in a Pay-Per-Click (PPC) campaign. In other words, you can look up how much advertisers will pay Google every time someone clicks on a link and generates a lead for that company. Certain keywords are worth more money than others. This is because the payoff is much higher for certain industries than others (a click for "health insurance" or "buy car" will be much higher than "hair brush" or "white socks"). This is because someone interested in buying health insurance or a car has the potential to spend A LOT more money than someone who might be interested in purchasing a hair brush or white socks.

So why is this information important to someone who is trying to make money online?

Well, with this information we have some very important metrics related to a keyword: how many searches there are per month for that keyword and what the value of that keyword is as a paid lead (also known as the Cost-Per-Click or CPC). We also know what percentage of traffic a #1 ranking in Google will bring on average: 42%. We also know how much Google pays it's publishers (i.e. the people who place their Google Adsense on their website): 68%. We also know the percentage of people who land on your website that will click on a paid link from Google on average (assuming good Ad placement): 4%.

So what can we do with all these numbers?

We can calculate the minimum amount of money a website can make monthly when it ranks for a specific keyword in Google. I say minimum because Google Adsense is generally the lowest money making method for monetizing a website online. It is also the easiest and that is why it is the introductory method I use, but once you become more experienced in making money online, you will learn other monetization methods that can make you much more money with the same amount of traffic to your websites.

So how do I calculate the amount of money a website can make if it ranks #1 for a specific keyword?

The formula is:

(Number of Searches) * (Cost Per Click) * (.42) * (.68) * (.04)

The .42 is the average percentage of visitors that will land on a website that ranks #1, the .68 is the percentage of earnings that Google will pay its publishers, and the .04 is the average percentage of people who will click on your website when they land on your page. So if for example, you look up the keyword "mountain bikes" and find that is searched for on average 45,000 times and has an average CPC of $1.00, this would be its monthly potential:

(45,000) * (1.00) * (.42) * (.68) * (.04) = $514.08

You would earn about $514.08 in passive income if your website ranked #1 in Google for "mountain bikes" and you put Google Adsense on your website. If you were to monetize with something like Amazon Associates, Ebay Affiliate Network, Commission Junction, or something else, your earnings could be much higher than that.

*Note: If you want to look up some keyword values in the Google Keyword Tool, be sure to look up the EXACT match keywords and not the BROAD match keywords (this is because we want to use only searches that type in that EXACT keyword, not keywords that includes those words or have some mix of them). Also be sure to use the GLOBAL average monthly searches instead of LOCAL (this is because we can drive traffic from all around the world to our website, not just our country).

So now you know the minimum amount of money you will make when you rank #1 in Google for any keyword by using this formula. To start playing around and doing a little research, check out the Google Keyword Tool: https://adwords.google.com/select/KeywordToolExternal . You can also watch a full free VIDEO lesson of me doing actual keyword research using the Google Keyword Tool: http://makemoneyfromhomelionsclub.com/lesson-2-1-how-to-do-keyword-research-for-free-using-the-google-keyword-tool/ .

UPDATE: I have uploaded a new second video on that page showing how to use the new Google Keyword Planner (Video Lesson 2.4), but be sure to watch BOTH videos entirely!

The next step is to figure out how competitive each keyword is by learning how to judge the current top 10 ranking websites for those keywords in Google's search results. You can do this by checking their PageRank. If you want to accurately figure out if YOU can rank a website for one of those keywords without too much work (because remember, if it's too much work, it's not worth it - easier keywords can be found), you can watch the free VIDEO lesson of me doing competition analysis for keywords using PageRank: http://makemoneyfromhomelionsclub.com/lions-club-2-2-how-to-do-competition-analysis-for-keywords-using-pagerank/ .

I hope you're starting to get an idea of how regular people ACTUALLY make online...by doing research BEFORE they make the website!

The Structure of a $1,000 per Month Passive Income Website

To understand the proper structuring of a $1,000 per month passive income website, you need to understand how Google ranks their websites.

Anyone who has ever heard of Google has probably heard of their "top-secret" algorithm that they use to sort their search results. Well the truth is that the foundation of that "top-secret" algorithm isn't very much of a secret at all (Want to know how everyone knows? Through Google search haha!).

The heart of Google's entire search engine algorithm is links. The more links a website has pointing to it from other websites, the more powerful and authoritative it is in Google's eyes. That's it...that is what it all boils down to. Sure, there are lots of other factors that make Google's results extra accurate and relevant (and a lot of those are still secret), but the number of backlinks to a website are the factor given the most weight.

So why does Google keep claiming that their search algorithm is much more complex than it actually is? Well, one of the main reasons is that it is in Google's best interest to keep their search engine inner-workings mysterious. For one, it keeps competing search engines from using their algorithms (Google is by far the most used search engine because it consistently gives the most relevant results, and they want to keep it that way). Another main reason is that Google doesn't want any websites trying to manipulate the system to gain a top ranking (remember from my earlier email how much more a #1 ranking is worth than a #5 or #10 ranking?).

Google is very against people trying to manipulate their rankings...they would rather all rankings be natural without anyone trying to artificially inflate their backlinks (this makes sense because they believe that the best results would be produced by the websites that naturally attract the most links). Unfortunately for Google, backlinks are the best way to judge a website's legitimacy and people who are in the business of making money online know this fact very well!

So you have better idea of how it all works, Google ranks each website by assigning it a number called PageRank. A PageRank can be anywhere between 0 and 10, with 10 being the highest possible rank. Google uses these numbers to give a rough assessment on how authoritative a website is, and generally websites with higher PageRank will rank higher in searches for more keywords.

Every time a website links to another website on the web, that means that the website is essentially giving a positive review of that other website. The more links a website has from different sources, the more authoritative that website becomes. Also, if a website with very high authority gives a link to a website with a much lower authority (i.e. - lower PageRank), that website will immediately gain credibility for having gained a link from an already credible site in Google's eyes. To put it plainly, the more links your website has, the better it will rank in Google (especially if some high PageRank websites have linked to your website).

And although Google cannot stop website owners from artificially inflating their PageRank and backlink profiles to get better rankings in searches, they can certainly make it more difficult or scary to do so. They do this by penalizing websites they suspect are engaging in that practice. This is known as black-hat search engine optimization (SEO) and Google has automatic triggers within its algorithm that will penalize websites that are caught doing black-hat SEO (essentially, shortcuts to gaining better rankings). A penalty can range from pushing your website to the last page of search results temporarily, to a complete deindexing of your website. A deindexing from Google pretty much means the death of a website, as you will never get any significant amount of organic traffic and all your work will be lost.

The practices I teach are white-hat SEO. These practices are the ones that Google encourages. They will bring you slower earnings and traffic numbers at the beginning, but they will make you the most amount of money over time. Not only that, they will safeguard your portfolio so you will never have to worry about penalties from Google (in fact, you will be rewarded in the long run). And trust me when I say you DO NOT want Google to notice that you have been messing around with black-hat SEO (I have friends who have lost website portfolios that were producing over $20,000/month because Google decided to deindex their portfolio due to shady link building practices...all at once).

Developing a steady-growth and passive income portfolio that will be safe and continue to grow for years and years is what my entire program is founded on, and all my free video lessons are founded on white-hat SEO link building practices (that is why the "get rich in 30 days online" Internet courses never work...they don't last long in Google).

So how does this knowledge relate to making a $1,000 per month passive income website? It's because I am going to show you how to structure a website and link building campaign so that each post ranks #1 for their target keyword. Each keyword chosen must have a potential passive earnings income of at least $50 per month, and the website will have at least 20 posts on it. $50 per month * 20 posts = $1,000.

Want to see how an example of how a white-hat SEO website is structured? Check out a fully Search Engine Optimized sample website that is designed to make $1,000 in passive income per month here: http://makemoneyfromhomesamplewebsite.com/. A full explanation video lesson of how this website was made (and why it was made this way!) can be found here: http://makemoneyfromhomelionsclub.com/lesson-3-1-how-to-make-a-2000-per-month-passive-income-website-using-onsite-seo-pt-1/. Obviously this lesson is relevant only AFTER you do your keyword research! But once you have, you are ready to make your first passive income website. ;)

The next part of the process is learning how to structure a link building campaign: http://makemoneyfromhomelionsclub.com/lesson-5-1-how-to-structure-a-link-building-campaign/. Remember, only white-hat SEO link building practices are taught for a safer portfolio and more money in the long run!

Also note that this passive income website is $1,000 per month because it is based on only 20 posts total. There's no reason not to make a website with 100 keyword researched posts. And then make 10 more of those websites.

Like so many things in life, making money online is a numbers game. More websites + more posts = more traffic = more money. THAT is the foundation of making money online.

I hope you have enjoyed my book! If so, please leave a positive review on Amazon.com and help spread the word!

This ebook was brought to you by http://makemoneyfromhomelionsclub.com.

If you are interested in entrepreneurship, making passive income online, and other ways to make money outside of a standard job, be sure to visit http://makemoneyfromhomelionsclub.com!

In the first video lesson you are taught the entire process of how http://mikeomarphotography.com was made from beginning to end, without the need of any coding knowledge, in under one hour!

With the lessons taught there, you will be able to make yourself a professional website with any kind of look that you want.

There are also lessons on Search Engine Optimization (SEO), social media promotion, making mailing lists, selling ebooks and other digital products, developing passive income online, and more. There are also lessons on how to make money with Google, Amazon, and ClickBank (all passive!).

Note: All of the links within this book can be found easily from my main website: http://makemoneyfromhomelionsclub.com

I love connecting with my readers and something I like to do is personally help them with their online financial goals.

I'd be happy to help you find success in any way that I can.

Please feel free to send me an email telling me who you are, why you are interested in making money online, what your online income goals are, and how you found out about my online school. You can email me via the "contact" page of the LIONS CLUB website.

You can find all of my ebooks at
http://makemoneyfromhomelionsclub.com/amazon

Mike Omar

My books:

HOW TO MAKE A WEBSITE OR BLOG: with WordPress WITHOUT Coding, on your own domain, all in under 2 hours.
http://makemoneyfromhomelionsclub.com/ebook1

HOW TO MAKE MONEY ONLINE: Learn how to make money from home with my step-by-step plan to build a $5000 per month passive income website portfolio (based on building 10 websites that make at least $500 per month each).
http://makemoneyfromhomelionsclub.com/ebook

HOW TO START A BLOG THAT PEOPLE WILL READ: How to create a website, write about a topic you love, develop a loyal readership, and make six figures doing it._
http://makemoneyfromhomelionsclub.com/ebookblog

All of the following websites were made using the exact same techniques outlined in this book and video lessons. Any of these websites will be within your ability to create once you complete the lessons:

Make Money from Home LIONS CLUB –
http://makemoneyfromhomelionsclub.com – My main website.

Mike Omar Photography – http://mikeomarphotography.com –
My freelancing website where I used to make websites for clients at $500 each (now it simply serves as an example website).

$1,000 / Month Passive Income Website –
http://makemoneyfromhomesamplewebsite.com - This is the structure and layout of a $1,000 / Month Passive Income website monetized with with Google Adsense and Amazon Associates.

Sample Sales Page – http://makemoneyfromhomeinfoproduct.com
– A samples sales page template that teaches how to make a website designed to sell a digital product.

How to Become a Ticket Broker –
http://howtobecomeaticketbroker.net - A live example of one of my passive income websites that makes money selling a digital product (an ebook).

High Quality Outsourcing – http://highqualityoutsourcing.com -
If you are interested in outsourcing the entire SEO backlinking process through my personal team (to get high rankings for your website(s) for specific keywords in Google and other searches), you can learn about that service here.

A few important things to keep in mind while reading through this book:

Throughout the book you will be referred to video lessons. While everything in the book and video lessons is as up to date as possible (I frequently update this book and the video lessons), the place to check for the most up-to-date information is in the *video descriptions* (on the same page you watch the videos). This can be the video descriptions on the pages of the LIONS CLUB website, or the video description of wherever you are watching the videos. Be sure to read the video descriptions of each video *before* watching the video itself.

Also, in this book you will find a lot of concepts are repeated. I know some readers will find this somewhat annoying, but several of my readers have told me they really like this because it really reinforces the most important concepts to take away from this book. That is why the book is written this way.

And most important of all: don't forget to sign up for my free weekly LIONS CLUB newsletter. Not only will you get great information with advice on how to make money online and how to build an online business, it is also where I send out updates regarding ranking strategies, new traffic generation techniques, important announcements, etc. Please sign up here:

http://makemoneyfromhomelionsclub.com/newsletter

Made in the USA
San Bernardino, CA
01 March 2016